THE STORY OF THE
ORLANDO MAGIC

THE NBA:
A HISTORY
OF HOOPS

THE STORY OF THE
ORLANDO
MAGIC

JIM WHITING

Published by Creative Paperbacks
P.O. Box 227, Mankato, Minnesota 56002
Creative Paperbacks is an imprint of
The Creative Company
www.thecreativecompany.us

Design and production by Blue Design
Art direction by Rita Marshall
Printed in the United States of America

Photographs by Corbis (Michael Martin/NewSport, Song
Qiong/Xinhua Press, ANDREW WALLACE/Reuters, JIM
YOUNG/Reuters), Getty Images (Andrew D. Bernstein/
NBAE, Nathaniel S. Butler/NBAE, Getty Images, Sam
Greenwood, Andy Hayt/NBAE, Yale Joel/Time & Life
Pictures, Chris McGrath, Fernando Medina/NBAE, Doug
Pensinger, Tony Ranze/AFP, Matt Stroshane), Newscom
(ERIK S. LESSER/EPA)

Library of Congress Cataloging-in-Publication Data
Whiting, Jim.
The story of the Orlando Magic / Jim Whiting.
p. cm. — (The NBA: a history of hoops)
Includes index.
Summary: An informative narration of the Orlando Magic
professional basketball team's history from its 1989
founding to today, spotlighting memorable players and
reliving dramatic events.
ISBN 978-1-60818-443-9 (hardcover)
ISBN 978-1-62832-029-9 (pbk)
1. Orlando Magic (Basketball team)—History—Juvenile
literature. I. Title.

GV885.52.O75W45 2014
796.323'640975924—dc23   2013039311

CCSS: RI.5.1, 2, 3, 8; RH.6-8.4, 5, 7

First Edition
9 8 7 6 5 4 3 2 1

Cover: Center Nikola Vucevic
Page 2: Guard Vince Carter
Pages 4-5: Forward DeQuan Jones (#20) & center Nikola
Vucevic (#9)
Page 6: Center Shaquille O'Neal

TABLE OF CONTENTS

COURTSIDE STORIES

INTRODUCING...

SORCERY IN THE SOUTH

WALT DISNEY WORLD'S EPCOT CENTER IS A POPULAR ORLANDO TOURIST ATTRACTION.

Like many American cities, Orlando, Florida, was first known under a different name: Jernigan, after Aaron Jernigan, the area's first settler. When he proved to be a terrible military leader in the mid-1850s, the town's leading citizens demanded a name change. Why they chose Orlando, however, is shrouded in mystery. The namesake could have been Orlando Reeves, a soldier supposedly killed in 1835 during the Second Seminole War—but an exhaustive search of military records years later found no one by that name. A second theory suggests that it was local cattle rancher Orlando Savage Rees. A third, more whimsical theory goes back to William Shakespeare's play *As You Like It*, in which the hero is named Orlando. One of the main thoroughfares in the city is Rosalind Avenue, purportedly after Rosalind, the play's quick-witted heroine.

In terms of what Orlando is today, the third explanation seems most fitting. Just as Shakespeare wrote to entertain the masses, so the city of Orlando aims to please. Nicknamed the "Theme Park Capital of the World," Orlando draws more than 50 million tourists every year to live out their dreams at attractions such as Universal Studios, SeaWorld, Gatorland, and Wet 'n Wild Water Park. But the city's first—and still best-known—theme park is Walt Disney World, which includes Epcot and the Magic Kingdom. Orlando is also home to another kind of Magic—its team in the National Basketball Association (NBA).

In 1986, a group led by businessman Jim Hewitt and former Philadelphia 76ers general manager Pat Williams began lobbying the NBA to give Orlando a franchise. Partnering with the *Orlando Sentinel*, they held a contest to name the team long before the NBA had made a decision. A committee chose "Magic" over three other finalists—"Tropics," "Juice," and "Heat." According to the committee, the name refers "to the magic of Orlando—a tourist hotspot with lots to offer visitors and those who called the area home."

In 1987, the league granted a franchise to Orlando. A year later, Williams hired former

THE LEAGUE EXPANDS

During the mid-1980s, the NBA decided to expand its then 23-team league by 3 franchises. In April 1987, the NBA Board of Governors granted Charlotte, North Carolina, a franchise to begin play in 1988 and Minneapolis, Minnesota, another one to start the following season. Two Florida cities—Orlando and Miami—vied for the third. Unable to choose just one, the NBA accepted both. The Miami Heat joined the league in 1988, and the Magic entered the next year. As they became a part of the league, the new teams rotated through the NBA's divisions. Orlando, despite its southern location, began as part of the Eastern Conference's Central Division. The team then moved into the Midwest Division and finally settled into the Atlantic Division for the 1991–92 season. "This rotating system will give the fans in these new franchise cities a chance to see all the NBA stars several times in the first three years," said league commissioner David Stern. When the teams at last migrated into their permanent geographic divisions, he said, they could "build rivalries with existing teams in the same area."

NICK ANDERSON

POSITION FORWARD / GUARD
HEIGHT 6-FOOT-6
MAGIC SEASONS
1989–99

Nick Anderson earned an honored place in Orlando's basketball story when the franchise selected him as its first pick (11th overall) in the 1989 NBA Draft. Entering the league out of the University of Illinois, Anderson was a versatile player who could swing between the forward and shooting guard positions. In both college and the pros, Anderson wore the number 25 on his jersey in honor of Ben Wilson, a high school basketball teammate who had been the victim of a senseless gang shooting. Over the course of 10 seasons in Orlando, Anderson established several franchise records, including games played (692), steals (1,004), and career points (10,650)—though Dwight Howard would soon eclipse the points standard. Although he wasn't as flashy or well-known as some of his Magic teammates, Anderson shone when playing alongside the likes of center Shaquille O'Neal and guard Penny Hardaway. Anderson took advantage of being in the shadows of his peers. "When other teams key on them and forget about me," he said, "then there's the dagger, right in the heart." In 2006, Anderson rejoined the Magic as a community ambassador for the team.

76ers coach Matt Guokas as the head coach for the inaugural 1989–90 season. "The opportunity to build something in two, three, four, five years is something I thought might be fun," Guokas said.

rlando's roster was built primarily through an expansion draft in which the Magic selected players from other NBA teams. Each team protected eight players, so Orlando was limited to those who were backups or past their prime. The Magic acquired players such as slick-shooting guard Reggie Theus, forwards Terry Catledge and Sidney Green, and scrappy point guard Scott Skiles. Orlando added to its roster by taking versatile University of Illinois swingman Nick Anderson with the 11th overall pick in the 1989 NBA Draft.

The Magic thrilled a sold-out Orlando Arena during their first preseason game, defeating the defending world champion Detroit Pistons 118–109. "We thought *we* were the defending champions after that game," said Magic guard Morlon Wiley. The Magic finished their first month in the NBA with a 7–7 record, the best-ever start by an expansion team. But the magic quickly faded. Despite a prolific offense, which ranked fifth in the NBA in total points, Orlando was the worst club defensively and ended the season 18–64.

With the fourth overall pick in the 1990 NBA Draft, the Magic selected sharpshooting forward Dennis Scott from Georgia Tech. Skiles improved his play during the 1990–91 season, setting a single-game record with 30 assists. "If any of those shots were missed, I would have fallen short, so I owe the record to my teammates," he said. The Magic's teamwork paid off, and Orlando jumped to 31–51.

The team slipped to 21–61 in the 1991–92 season, but fans still turned out to show their support, selling out all 41 home games. Despite all the losses, there was a silver lining. The poor record put Orlando in position to make an addition to the team that would dramatically brighten its future.

SCOTT SKILES

POSITION GUARD
HEIGHT 6-FOOT-1
MAGIC SEASONS
1989–94

The Magic selected Scott Skiles from the Indiana Pacers' roster during the NBA's 1989 expansion draft. Known for his durability and gritty style of play, the point guard quickly became a fan favorite in Orlando, and during his Magic years, he was a nearly permanent fixture in every game. During the 1992–93 season, Skiles averaged 39.6 minutes of on-court time per game, third-most in the league. At 6-foot-1, Skiles was smaller than most NBA players, but he also played with greater intensity and self-confidence than most of his opponents. "I played more of a tough kind of game," he said later, "but I had no choice. That was the only way I could play in order to survive and have a career." A team leader, Skiles poured his energy into motivating his teammates and became at that time the Magic's all-time leader in assists, with 2,776. In a victory over the Nuggets on December 30, 1990, he set a still-standing single-game NBA record with 30 assists. Skiles later became head coach of the Phoenix Suns, Chicago Bulls, and Milwaukee Bucks.

BUILDING AROUND SHAQ

SHAQUILLE O'NEAL WAS THE FIRST ROOKIE NBA ALL-STAR SINCE MICHAEL JORDAN.

The grand prize of the 1992 NBA Draft was Shaquille O'Neal, a 7-foot-1 and 300-pound center from Louisiana State University, whose rare combination of size and strength had scouts predicting instant stardom. With 10 chances out of 66 in the draft lottery drawing, Orlando won the top pick and the young giant known as "Shaq." In his first year, O'Neal averaged 23.4 points, 13.9 rebounds, and 3.5 blocked shots. "There's no doubt he's going to be a monster," said Miami Heat center Rony Seikaly. "He palms the ball like a grapefruit." Voted NBA Rookie of the Year, Shaq led the Magic to a respectable 41–41 mark, and Orlando missed the playoffs by the narrowest of margins. After the season, assistant coach Brian Hill became head coach.

With the best record among the league's non-playoff teams in 1992–93, the Magic had a 1-in-66 chance of

DENNIS SCOTT

POSITION FORWARD
HEIGHT 6-FOOT-8
MAGIC SEASONS
1990–97

After leaving college early to enter the 1990 NBA Draft, Dennis Scott was selected fourth overall by the Magic and quickly made his mark. During his first game, Scott drained three three-pointers in a three-minute span while wearing jersey number 3—a debut performance that earned him the nickname "3-D." Scott's charismatic style and flashy smile gained him a large fan following, and he became known around the league for his long-distance shooting. "I just thank God every day for my personality and my jump shot," Scott once said. The forward went on to knock down 125 three-pointers during the 1990–91 season, which, at the time, was the best long-range production by a rookie in league history. Five years later, he made hoops history again when he finished the 1995–96 season with 267 three-pointers, an NBA single-season record that stood until 2006. When he was not playing basketball, the sharpshooter was talking about it. Scott enjoyed being in front of the camera, and during his time in Orlando, he hosted two television programs: *The Dennis Scott Show* and *The Highlight Zone*.

"I'M GLAD I'M GETTING OUT OF THIS GAME SOON.
I DON'T WANT TO BE AROUND WHEN THOSE TWO
GROW UP."

— JAMES WORTHY ON HARDAWAY AND O'NEAL

obtaining the top pick in the 1993 Draft. Yet Orlando again won the number-one choice. The Magic chose brawny forward Chris Webber, and then traded his rights for Memphis State point guard Anfernee "Penny" Hardaway and three future first-round picks.

t 6-foot-7, Hardaway was taller than most point guards, yet he had the quickness and ball-handling ability to slash to the basket. With Hardaway and O'Neal, the Magic suddenly had one of the league's most potent and promising duos. "I'm glad I'm getting out of this game soon," said Los Angeles Lakers forward James Worthy. "I don't want to be around when those two grow up."

In 1993–94, O'Neal and Hardaway led the Magic to a 50–32 record, finishing second in the Eastern Conference's Atlantic Division. Although the Indiana Pacers swept the Magic in the first round of the playoffs, it was evident that Orlando was a team on the rise.

One reason for the Magic's quick postseason exit was the lack of a strong forward. In the off-season, Orlando added 6-foot-10 forward Horace Grant, a powerful defender who had won three NBA championships with the Chicago Bulls. Orlando also welcomed point guard Brian Shaw, formerly with the Heat. Shaw soon became half of the so-called "Shaw-Shaq Redemption," a crowd-pleasing, alley-oop pass play from Shaw to Shaq. When Scott sat out with a back injury, quick forward Donald Royal effectively filled in. The 1994–95 Magic finished with the best mark (57–25) in the conference. In the playoffs, the Magic powered past the Boston Celtics, the Bulls, and the Pacers to advance to the NBA Finals, where they faced star center Hakeem Olajuwon and the defending champion Houston Rockets. The Rockets were too much for the Magic to handle, though, and swept Orlando in four games.

The Magic returned with a vengeance in 1995–96. Orlando started 17–5, propelled in part by the long-range gunning of Scott, who set an NBA record with 267 three-pointers during the season. Orlando finished 60–22 and advanced to the Eastern Conference finals. But the Bulls— who featured superstar guard Michael Jordan— swept Orlando in four games.

A BACKBOARD-BREAKING YEAR

During his first year in the NBA, center Shaquille O'Neal announced his arrival by declaring war on the league's backboards. On February 7, 1993, Shaq slammed a ferocious dunk at America West Arena in Phoenix, and then hung on the rim, pulling the backboard forward. The back end of the base lifted off the ground, and the collapsible basket folded into its storage position. The spectacle delayed the game 35 minutes while crews repaired the basket. Orlando lost the game 121–105, but O'Neal's dunk was the news of the night. Almost three months later in New Jersey, Shaq struck again with a power dunk against the Nets that ripped apart the backboard's support braces. The backboard, stanchion, and base all had to be replaced, delaying the game for more than 45 minutes. Fortunately, the arena had an extra backboard to replace the broken pieces, and the Magic managed a 119–116 victory. "It really came crashing down," O'Neal said afterward. "The shot clock hit me in the head. It hurt a little bit, but not that much. I have a hard head."

A MAGIC PENNY

PENNY HARDAWAY KEPT DEFENDERS OFF BALANCE WITH HIS QUICK PASSES AND CUTS.

rlando fans were heartbroken when O'Neal left the Magic in the summer of 1996 to chase higher-profile stardom in Los Angeles with the Lakers. The team's fate now rested squarely on Hardaway's shoulders. "It's Penny's team now," said Grant, "and we'll go as far as he takes us."

Before the 1996–97 season, the Magic acquired veteran center Rony Seikaly—one of the best rebounders in the game—to help fill the void left by O'Neal. Although a knee injury sidelined Hardaway, Seikaly averaged 17.3 points and 9.5 boards. Late in the season, coach Hill was fired and replaced by assistant Richie Adubato. The Magic finished 45–37, good enough for a spot in the playoffs.

In the first round, Orlando faced off against the Heat, who crushed the Magic in the first two games. Orlando showed signs of life in Game 3 when 6-foot point guard

THE ROAD TO THE FINALS

In the 1995 playoffs, the fast-rising Magic swept the Boston Celtics in four games in the first round before facing the Chicago Bulls. With Orlando trailing late in the fourth quarter of Game 1, swingman Nick Anderson poked the ball away from Chicago guard Michael Jordan. Magic guard Penny Hardaway grabbed the loose ball, drove down the court, and passed to forward Horace Grant, who slammed home the game-winning basket with 6.2 seconds remaining. The Magic went on to clinch the series in six games. Next, Orlando faced the Indiana Pacers in the Eastern Conference finals, which went a full seven games. The Magic exploded in the third quarter of Game 7, pulling ahead by 19 points, and held on for the victory. In the NBA Finals, the Magic met the Houston Rockets, who came back from a 20-point, second-quarter deficit in Game 1 to pull out a 120–118 overtime victory. The deflated Magic then lost the next three games in a series sweep. "It's a hard loss to take," center Shaquille O'Neal said. "I thought this was our year."

Darrell Armstrong—a backup during the regular season—sparked the team, scoring 21 points and allowing Hardaway to swing to shooting guard. Hardaway poured in 42 points of his own, and the Magic took the game, 88–75. "It's one of the best performances I've ever seen Penny have since I've been here," said Adubato. Hardaway followed up that performance with 41 points in Game 4, leading Orlando to another victory. In

Game 5, however, the Heat held on for a 91–83 win to take the game and the series.

The next season, former Pistons coach Chuck Daly came to Orlando as the Magic's new bench leader. Injuries to Hardaway and Anderson crippled the team's title hopes in 1997–98, yet Armstrong and hardworking forwards Derek Strong and Charles "Bo" Outlaw led the Magic to a respectable 41–41 finish.

AT 6-FOOT-11, RONY SEIKALY POWERED HIS WAY INSIDE ON BOTH ENDS OF THE FLOOR.

TRACY McGRADY

T-MAC PUTS ON A SHOW

When Tracy McGrady scored seven points in the first quarter against the Washington Wizards on March 10, 2004, no one could have foreseen what would happen. "T-Mac" began pouring in the points, mostly on midrange jumpers, and finished the first half with 28. He did even better in the third quarter, notching 24. "My teammates came to me and told me to get 60, then they told me to get 70," McGrady said. Though just the 17th player in NBA history to notch 60 points, he had a golden opportunity to become only the fifth to score 70 or more. But he went cold in the fourth quarter, missing 10 of his last 11 shots and finishing with 62. He also missed nine free throws during the game. "I was fresh the whole game," said McGrady. "It was just when you get to a point where you are about to break records, break your career high, break the Magic single-game high, all those things get in your head." Nonetheless, Los Angeles Lakers guard Kobe Bryant has been the only man to score more points in a game since T-Mac's historic night.

"IT'S A BIG DISAPPOINTMENT. I THOUGHT WE WERE A BETTER TEAM THAN THIS."

— NICK ANDERSON ON THE PLAYOFF LOSS TO THE 76ERS

In the 1998 NBA Draft, the Magic used two first-round selections to pick up bruising forward Matt Harpring and center Michael Doleac. Daly's second season as Orlando's coach was shortened to 50 games because of a dispute between NBA players and owners. After the 1998–99 season finally opened in February, the Magic bolted to a 33–17 record, and then met the 76ers in the playoffs. The teams split the first two games, but star guard Allen Iverson led the 76ers to convincing victories in Games 3 and 4. "It's a big disappointment," Anderson said. "I thought we were a better team than this." After the season, Daly retired, and Hardaway asked to be traded.

n 1999, after Hardaway was sent to the Suns for two forwards—outside shooter Pat Garrity and savvy veteran Danny Manning—and two future first-round draft picks, the Magic hired former NBA guard Glenn "Doc" Rivers as head coach. Rivers's low-key style was the perfect tonic for the young Magic. With a roster devoid of superstars (five players had not even been selected in the NBA Draft), Orlando was predicted by nearly every preseason publication to finish near the bottom of the league.

Facing such negativity, the team adopted the slogan "Heart and Hustle," which described the group's hardworking and dedicated attitude. This determination helped the Magic to overachieve on almost every level. With Armstrong, Outlaw, smart center John Amaechi, and brawny forward Ben Wallace forming the core, the Magic went 41–41, missing the playoffs by a single game. Rivers was named NBA Coach of the Year, just the fifth rookie head coach to claim the trophy.

INTRODUCING...

SHAQUILLE O'NEAL

**POSITION CENTER
HEIGHT 7-FOOT-1
MAGIC SEASONS
1992–96**

As a freshman at Louisiana State University, Shaquille O'Neal measured 6-foot-11, but he still wasn't done growing. Three years later, he had added two more inches and won the Adolph Rupp trophy, presented to college basketball's top player. The NBA welcomed him via the 1992 Draft, when Orlando grabbed him with the top overall selection. Despite his imposing size, "Shaq" projected the image of a gentle giant, arriving for his new job in Orlando wearing Mickey Mouse ears. "He's a combination of the Terminator and Bambi," said O'Neal's agent, Leonard Armato. O'Neal was an instant success with the Magic as well as in the commercial market. Throughout his career, he acquired several nicknames, including "Big Diesel," which compared Shaq to a powerful engine, and "Big Aristotle," which referred to his commitment to sharp mental focus. His mere presence on the court was enough to change the game. Opponents usually double- or even triple-teamed O'Neal, leaving his teammates with more opportunities to score. After he left Orlando, O'Neal went on to win three NBA championships with the Lakers and one with the Heat.

T-MAC TAKES OVER

THE MAGIC LOOKED TO DYNAMITE SCORER TRACY McGRADY FOR A PLAYOFFS PUSH.

The Magic made headlines in 2000 by signing both superstar forward Grant Hill and explosive swingman Tracy McGrady to free-agent contracts. Orlando then added another potent scorer by selecting 6-foot-8 guard/forward Mike Miller, known for his three-point-range marksmanship, with the fifth overall pick in the NBA Draft. "Last year, we built a nucleus of guys that work hard every night and do the little things," explained Coach Rivers. "Now, with the addition of Hill and McGrady, we have the weapons necessary to win the big games."

McGrady, known to fans as "T-Mac," made an immediate impact, scoring a career-high 32 points in the first game. Hill, however, suffered from a lingering ankle injury, which kept him out of all but four games of the 2000–01 season. Despite Hill's absence, Rivers guided his young team to a 43–39 record. Miller set a new franchise record for the

MIKE MILLER'S LETHAL
PERIMETER SHOOTING MADE
HIM ROOKIE OF THE YEAR
IN 2001.

most three-pointers made by a rookie (148) and won the 2001 NBA Rookie of the Year award. With McGrady averaging 26.8 points and 7.5 rebounds a game, the Magic made the playoffs for the 6th time in 8 years.

Magic fans were deflated as their team lost the first two games of the opening-round series to the Milwaukee Bucks. T-Mac gave them hope in Game 3, scoring 42 points to boost Orlando to a 121–116 overtime victory. But the Magic could not hold on to that momentum, and the Bucks bounced them out of the series in Game 4.

McGrady became a true NBA superstar the next season, as he and Lakers guard Kobe Bryant were the only 2 players in the league to average at least 25 points, 5 rebounds, and 5 assists per game. McGrady and the Magic played particularly well at home, going 27–14. With solid play from Grant, Armstrong, and Miller, the Magic finished 44–38 and met Charlotte in the first round of the playoffs. With several players injured by season's end, the team hobbled through the series (with McGrady taking breaks to lie on the floor to soothe his sore back) and was defeated by the Hornets in four games.

ANFERNEE "PENNY" HARDAWAY

POSITION GUARD
HEIGHT 6-FOOT-7
MAGIC SEASONS
1993–99

When Anfernee Hardaway was a child, he lived with his grandmother, who often called him "pretty." With her thick Southern accent, the name sounded more like "Penny," and Hardaway's friends soon began calling him Penny, too. The third overall pick in the 1993 NBA Draft, Hardaway joined the Magic through a post-draft trade that sent forward Chris Webber from Orlando to Golden State. Alongside superstar center Shaquille O'Neal, Hardaway became an instant sensation. As a rookie, he averaged 16 points per game and came a close second to Webber in Rookie of the Year award voting. Fans and coaches likened Hardaway to Lakers star Magic Johnson, as both were taller than most point guards yet still excelled at handling the ball. Hardaway's unique combination of size and skill made him too big for most point guards to defend and too fast for many shooting guards to keep up with. "I can see why people compare him to Magic," said Orlando forward Dennis Scott. "He does whatever he feels the team needs, and that's what makes him the All-Star he is."

In 2002–03, two newcomers, sharpshooting guard Gordan Giricek and scrappy forward Drew Gooden, helped Orlando to finish 42–40—the 11th straight year in which the franchise finished .500 or better. Facing the top-seeded Pistons in the Eastern Conference playoffs, McGrady started the series with a bang, going for 43 and then 46 points respectively in the first 2 games. But after taking a three-games-to-one lead, Orlando broke down. McGrady could not shoulder the entire burden, and the Pistons fought back to win the series in seven games. "I can't win it by myself," T-Mac said. "I'm pretty sure [my teammates] understand that."

Orlando began the 2003–04 campaign with an overtime win over the New York Knicks, but the season crumbled as the team lost the next 19 games. T-Mac continued to shine, setting a new franchise record with a 62-point game in a win over the Washington Wizards and becoming the second-youngest player (after Kobe Bryant) to reach 10,000 career points. Despite these highlights, Orlando plummeted to a league-worst 21–61 record. Frustrated by the poor season and the team's continuing playoff struggles, McGrady asked to be traded. Orlando sent him to the Rockets for quick guard Steve Francis, and the Magic embarked on another rebuilding project.

STEVE FRANCIS WASN'T HAPPY WITH HIS ORLANDO TRADE AT FIRST BUT SOON FOUND A GROOVE.

STUFF, THE MAGIC MASCOT

Even before the Magic played their first game, Orlando's mascot—Stuff the Magic Dragon—was born ... or, more accurately, hatched. On October 27, 1988, a large egg appeared in front of the Magic's stadium, the Orlando Arena, or the "O-Rena." The egg exploded into a shower of deflated basketballs, bumper stickers, and puffs of green smoke. A tall, fuzzy green dragon with a pink-and-blue Mohawk and a five-foot wingspan emerged. Appropriately, Stuff made his community debut on Halloween that year at Church Street Station. Since then, Stuff has become one of the most recognizable mascots in professional sports. The dragon represents the Magic at every home game, and his antics and energy have earned him a large fan base of all ages. Stuff also attends Magic-related activities and civic and social events in central Florida. Stuff's favorite sayings include "Dragon my heels, but gotta fly" and "Stuff it!" To help entertain the crowds, Stuff enlists two sidekicks, the inflatable Air Stuff and the small Mini Stuff, who occasionally appear with the original dragon.

DWIGHT HOWARD TO THE RESCUE

FORWARD RASHARD LEWIS GAINED A REPUTATION FOR HIS POSTSEASON SHARPSHOOTING.

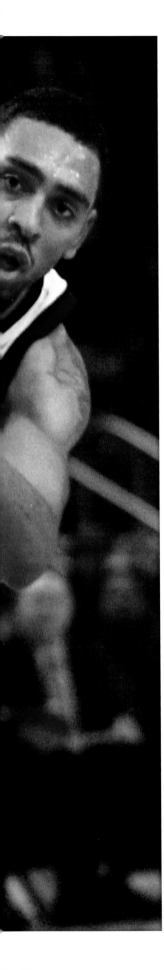

Before the 2004–05 season, the Magic hit the lottery jackpot for the third time, winning the top selection in the 2004 NBA Draft. Orlando chose 6-foot-11 center Dwight Howard, a high school superstar from Atlanta, Georgia, who won the 2004 Naismith Award as the nation's top high school player. The Magic also acquired rookie guard Jameer Nelson in a draft-night trade. Before the start of the season, free-agent forwards Tony Battie and Turkish-born Hedo Turkoglu were also decked out in Orlando blue and white.

The retooled Magic started the season 13–7. The quick and confident Francis led the team with 21.3 points per game. Hill, who had endured years of ankle pain and undergone several surgeries, finally returned to top form, averaging 19.7 points. Although the Magic finished the season 36–46, optimism was rising again in Orlando.

BETWEEN HIS ORLANDO COACHING STINTS, BRIAN HILL LED THE STRUGGLING VANCOUVER GRIZZLIES.

"We've got something to look forward to next year," said Howard.

Orlando brought back a familiar face as head coach—Brian Hill, who had led the Magic to 3 seasons of 50-plus wins in the 1990s. As the Magic started a disappointing 20–40 in 2005–06, the year's biggest highlight came from the 19-year-old Howard, who became the youngest player to notch a "20-20 game," with 21 points and 20 rebounds against the recently established Charlotte Bobcats. The team pulled together to win 16 of its last 22 games to finish with the same record as the previous year.

Despite ranking near the bottom of the league in turnovers, the Magic mustered a 40–42 mark in 2006–07. Orlando returned to the postseason for the first time in four years, but the Pistons made short work of the Magic, sweeping the series in four games. Shortly after that, Stan Van Gundy, a former Heat head coach, took over in Orlando. The Magic then signed free-agent forward Rashard Lewis, an athletic and reliable scorer.

The 2007–08 Magic vaulted to a 52–30 mark, their best since 1995-96. "We've had a good season," said Lewis, "but we know we have to win in the playoffs to get a little more respect." Win they did, defeating the Toronto Raptors in five games in the first round. Howard led the way with three 20-20 games. "To finally get over the hump and get out of the first round, it means a lot," said Howard. But the Pistons bounced Orlando in the second round.

In the off-season, Orlando focused on placing new talent around its young center, signing swingman Mickael Pietrus as a free agent and nabbing Courtney Lee—a sweet-shooting guard from Western Kentucky University—in the 2008

DWIGHT HOWARD

POSITION CENTER
HEIGHT 6-FOOT-11
MAGIC SEASONS
2004–12

As an eighth-grader, Dwight Howard set a personal goal to be the top selection in the NBA Draft. After graduating from Southwest Atlanta Christian Academy in 2004, Howard fulfilled that goal and became just the third player to be the top overall selection in the NBA Draft straight out of high school. The Magic immediately made him a starter. With his size, speed, and power, Howard was 1 of only 8 players to average a double-double in 2004–05, netting 12 points and grabbing 10 rebounds per game. "He's just genetically superior to most people from a physical standpoint," said Orlando strength and conditioning coach Joe Rogowski. Howard showed he was still a big kid during the 2008 All-Star Game weekend's Slam Dunk Contest, which he won while flying through the air wearing a Superman cape. In 2008, Howard said that during his first few years in the NBA, "the biggest thing was being on ESPN highlights. Now, it's seeing my team win." Unfortunately for Magic fans, his team became the Los Angeles Lakers as the result of a 2012 trade.

FORWARD BRANDON BASS AVERAGED 11.2 POINTS PER GAME IN 2010–11.

LOTTERY MAGIC

The annual NBA Draft lottery determines the order in which non-playoff teams get to draft players. During its first 20 years, Orlando beat the odds and won the number-one pick 3 times. In 1991–92, the Magic finished with the second-worst record in the league. The 11 teams with the worst marks were eligible for the lottery, which involved putting a total of 66 Ping-Pong balls in a drum. Holding 10 of the balls, the Magic had a 15.2 percent chance at the top pick. Orlando won the lottery and drafted center Shaquille O'Neal. The following year, the Magic just missed the playoffs. Having only one Ping-Pong ball in the 1993 lottery, they defied the odds to win the top spot again, and then pulled a trade to acquire guard Anfernee "Penny" Hardaway. Orlando's third win came in 2004, when the team had the worst record and the most balls in the drum. "We suffered for every one of those balls," said Orlando general manager Pat Williams. "I'm just glad they did their job." With the top pick, the Magic selected high school center Dwight Howard.

NBA Draft. The Magic started out hot, buoyed by Howard's first career triple-double—30 points, 19 rebounds, and 10 blocked shots in a single game. When Nelson suffered a season-ending shoulder injury, the Magic acquired speedy point guard Rafer Alston as a replacement.

Alston kept the offense running smoothly as Orlando embarked on an eye-opening postseason run. It roared all the way to the NBA Finals by toppling the 76ers, the defending champion Celtics, and the high-powered Cleveland Cavaliers. The Magic could not quite reach the top of the mountain, though, losing to the Lakers in the Finals. A similar story played out in 2009–10. After adding All-Star swingman Vince Carter, the Magic's season was quashed by the Celtics in the conference finals.

The team dropped to 52–30 in 2010–11, and lost in the first round of the playoffs to the Atlanta Hawks, four games to two. Howard was named the league's Defensive Player of the Year for the third straight time. But as a team, the Magic continued to decline in the lockout-shortened 2011–12 season, playing in the shadow of Howard's demands to be traded. Though he became less vocal as the season progressed, Howard then underwent back surgery and missed the final games. Orlando made an early exit from the playoffs, winning just one game in a series against the Pacers.

The off-season was tumultuous, as Van Gundy left the organization after compiling a 259–135 regular-season record and leading the team to the playoffs during each of his five years at the helm. He was replaced by San Antonio assistant coach Jacque Vaughn. Then the "Dwightmare" continued when Howard again asked to be traded. He eventually went to the Lakers in a complicated four-team trade that brought six

players and several draft choices to Orlando. The team also added 6-foot-9 Canadian power forward Andrew Nicholson from St. Bonaventure University with its top pick in the 2012 NBA Draft. As the smoke from all the wheeling and dealing cleared, Orlando's general manager Rob Hennigan took a realistic look at the roster. "Are we taking a step back?" he said. "Absolutely, we are. But we're taking a step back with a vision."

Unfortunately, Hennigan was right about the "step back." The Magic finished 2012–13 with an NBA-worst 20–62 mark. On the positive side, 6-foot-9 rookie center Nikola Vucevic grabbed a franchise-record 29 rebounds in a New Year's Eve contest, and his 11.9 rebounds per game ranked second in the NBA. Nelson's 413 assists vaulted him past Scott Skiles to a Magic career-record 3,025 assists. "We feel good about how we're positioned for the future," Hennigan said. "We believe we will get better, and I think that the group that we were able to establish this season is a really good starting point for that."

The 2013–14 season proved that success wouldn't come overnight. Orlando received a welcome addition in dynamic guard Victor Oladipo, who slowly developed an offensive rhythm with Vucevic and forward Tobias Harris. But the Magic finished in the basement of the Eastern Conference.

So even though the team remains in a rebuilding mode, its past provides Orlando fans with plenty of reasons to be optimistic. With a history of 14 postseason appearances in just 24 years of existence, the Magic have demonstrated that their success stems from much more than pulling rabbits out of hats.

INDEX